Travel
Transport

Neil Morris

Belitha Press

First published in the UK in 1999 by

Belitha Press Limited, London House,
Great Eastern Wharf, Parkgate Road,
London SW11 4NQ

Text © copyright Neil Morris 1999

Text in this format © copyright Belitha Press Ltd 1999

ISBN 1 85561 889 3

British Library Cataloguing in Publication Data for this
book is available from the British Library.

Series editor: Honor Head
Series designer: Jamie Asher
Picture researcher: Diana Morris
Consultant: Sallie Purkis

Printed in Singapore

9 8 7 6 5 4 3 2 1

Picture Credits

Hulton Getty: front cover b, 4t, 8, 10, 11t, 11c, 12, 13t, 13b,
14, 16, 17t, 19t, 21t, 22t, 24, 25t, 25b, 28.
Peter Newark's Pictures: 6, 7t, 15b, 18.
Public Record Office: front cover t & c, back cover, 1, 2, 4b,
5t, 5b, 7c, 7b, 9t, 9c, 9b, 11b, 13c, 15t, 17b, 19b, 20, 21c,
21b, 22b, 23t, 23b, 26t, 26b, 27t, 27b, 29t, 29b.

Words in **bold** are in the glossary on page 30.

CONTENTS

Introduction	4
Horsepower	6
In Town	8
Rivers and Canals	10
The Railways	12
Isambard K Brunel	14
Ships	16
Postal Service	18
The Omnibus	20
Bicycles	22
The Underground	24
Rail Network	26
Horseless Carriages	28
Glossary	30
Index	32

INTRODUCTION

During Victorian times horse-drawn transport was very important. Stagecoaches ran on Britain's main roads, carrying passengers on long journeys and delivering the mail. Towns were full of horse-drawn carriages, but dramatic developments were taking place. Omnibuses and trams became a familiar sight in cities and more people began to ride bicycles. But the biggest changes were brought about by the coming of the railways and the new steam train.

We use the word Victorian to describe the time when Queen Victoria was on the British throne. Born in 1819, Victoria was the only child of Edward, the fourth son of King George III, and Victoria Maria Louisa, the daughter of a German duke. She became queen in 1837, and three years later married Albert, a German prince. They had nine children before Albert died in 1861. Victoria ruled for almost 64 years, longer than any other British monarch. She died in 1901.

When Victoria came to the throne, there were already a few railway lines. During her reign a vast rail network spread across the whole country, so that by 1901 most towns and many villages had railway stations. Rail companies built new towns, and existing towns grew at a fast pace. Crewe, for example, was an important railway town. In 1837 around 200 people lived there, but by 1901 it had a population of more than 42 000.

By the end of the nineteenth century, Britain's large cities were already full of carriages, omnibuses and trams. This was particularly true in London, though there the situation was helped by the underground railway, which had been running beneath the streets for some years. But the next transport revolution was just around the corner – the horseless carriage or motor car.

HORSEPOWER

For short journeys in both town and country, most early Victorians travelled around on their own two feet. Children and adults walked everywhere, but people then didn't travel as far afield as people do today. Most people only ever left their home town, village or county to look for work.

Before the arrival of the railways, the only real alternative to **shanks' pony** was to ride a horse or ride in a carriage pulled along by horses. Horses were used for pulling goods as well as passengers. Though steam and petrol engines brought trains and the first cars into everyday use before the end of the nineteenth century, horse-drawn travel was still extremely important at the end of Queen Victoria's reign.

The improvement of roads helped horse-drawn travel. Just before Victoria became queen, a Scottish engineer named John Loudon McAdam had developed a type of road surface which came to be known as macadam. He realized that ordinary soil, if it was well prepared, drained and protected, could take the weight of traffic without having an expensive layer of rock. His roads were made of layers of small, crushed stones and gravel packed over soil.

▼ *Before there were any trains or buses to catch, the cheapest way to travel was by carrier's wagon. The covered wagons were mainly built to carry goods and parcels. The wheels were wide, but the wagons were not very comfortable for people to ride in.*

◄ *Stagecoaches often ran with teams of four fast horses. They carried passengers and their luggage on long journeys, breaking them up into stages. Because of the poor state of the roads, the ride could be very bumpy! As roads improved, **tolls** were charged to use them. The coachman had to stop at each toll gate and pay to go through.*

► *This open carriage, called a brake, is leaving a stop at an inn. Horses were normally changed at these coaching inns, or coach houses. New passengers could also join the coach there. They could have food and drink while they waited for the coach to arrive or for the horses to be changed. Poorer people would sometimes hire a horse and carriage for a special event, such as a wedding.*

► *Horses were traditionally used for all sorts of farm work. They were used to carry crops as well as to transport the farmer and his workers. This cart has a full load of hay. Horses and carts were used in towns too, for delivering goods to people. Coal, bread and milk were all delivered by horse and cart.*

IN TOWN

Horse-drawn transport was popular among richer people for short journeys in town. Those who could afford them had their own private carriages. Others found it more convenient to hire hackney carriages, horse-drawn cabs which were used as taxis. In large towns and cities, cabs began to wait outside railway stations and theatres, ready for hire, just as mini-cabs and taxis do today.

During Victorian times most forms of transport were quite slow, especially in the towns. People expected journeys to take much longer than we would today, and so they made time for them. Travellers also had to be more patient because there were no road markings, no road signs and certainly no traffic lights. Drivers followed the British rule of the road by driving on the left.

▼ *This engraving shows the Carriage Department at the Great Exhibition of 1851. The exhibition, which was held in London's Hyde Park, displayed more than 100 000 **industrial** exhibits from all over the world. The carriages were made by companies from all over Britain, and they* *included **invalid** carriages and **hearses**. Some of them were fitted with a device that could tell the owner how many miles the carriage had travelled every day. This was a useful way of checking up on staff and making sure that the owners' horses were not driven too hard.*

◄ A hansom cab waits for passengers in London. This type of two-wheeled carriage could carry two inside the closed cab, with the driver seated behind. It was named after Joseph Hansom (1803-82), an English architect, who designed and **patented** it in 1834. By the end of the nineteenth century there were 7000 hansoms in London alone.

◄ This advertisement of 1896 shows how important horse travel still was towards the end of the century. Many different vehicles are shown and listed, including two-wheeled **traps**.

► This photograph of Oxford Circus, London, was taken in 1888. It shows how crowded the capital's streets had become. There are all sorts of horse-drawn carts and carriages, carrying passengers and goods.

RIVERS AND CANALS

During early Victorian times, before the new railway lines spread throughout the country, it was difficult to transport goods across land. But there was an alternative: Britain's waterways. By the end of the eighteenth century, many canals had been built which joined rivers across the land.

The men who dug the canals and laid new roads and new rail track were known as navvies, short for navigators. In the early days, before the widespread use of the steam engine, navvies used to dig out the earth with spades. By 1860, there were more than 3000 kilometres of canals in Britain.

Locks were designed and built to move boats on the canals from one level to another. But the Victorians were always looking for new solutions to engineering problems. In 1875 a huge boat lift began operating at Anderton, in Cheshire. This **hydraulic** lift raised boats over 15 metres from the River Weaver to the Trent and Mersey Canal. It did the same job as a row of ten locks.

◄ *Until about 1880 most canal barges were pulled by horses. The horse walked on a path beside the canal and towed the barge along by rope. This is why paths beside rivers and canals are called towpaths. From the 1880s, many canal boats were powered by steam engines.*

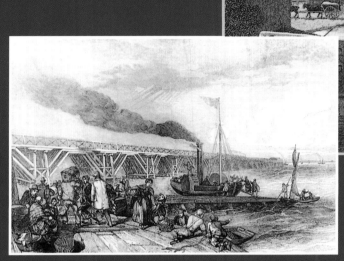

▲ Narrow boats were specially designed for canals. These two are moving out of a lock on the Regent's Canal, in London. Boats still travel along this canal between the Grand Union Canal and the River Thames. It has a series of 12 locks which take boats up to a higher level or down to a lower level. A boat moves into the lock and the gates close. The lock then fills with water, taking the boat up to the next level, or empties, taking the boat down.

▲ People used a **paddle-steamer** ferry to cross the River Humber, as this illustration of 1848 shows. Road and footbridges were not common at this time, though many railway bridges were being built. You can see a railway bridge in the background. This ferry was run by a railway company.

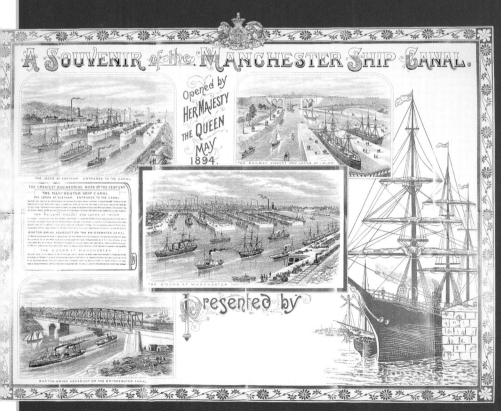

◀ The Manchester Ship Canal opened in 1894. This canal was a huge engineering success. It is 58 kilometres long, over 36 metres wide, and at least 6.7 metres deep. It connects the city of Manchester with the mouth of the River Mersey and the Irish Sea. When it opened, it made Manchester an inland **port** and was used by the cotton textile industry to move goods around more easily.

THE RAILWAYS

The world's very first railway trains steamed along in Britain during the early nineteenth century. The first public train ran in 1825, on the Stockton and Darlington Railway in north-east England. By 1840 lines had been extended to connect Liverpool, Manchester and London.

The new railways changed the way people thought about travel. The more successful the railways were, the cheaper it became for rail companies to build more tracks and put on more trains. By 1848 about 8000 kilometres of track had been laid in Britain, along with **cuttings**, **embankments**, tunnels, bridges and **viaducts**. People and goods could move around the country much faster, more cheaply and in some comfort.

There were usually three classes of travel. First-class passengers travelled in closed carriages, while second and third class were often open. In 1844 the government ordered the railway companies to improve their services. They had to put roofs on third-class carriages on normal services, but most carriages still had no form of lighting.

► *George Stephenson (1781-1848) and his son Robert (1803-59), at work in their cottage. George Stephenson built his first steam* **locomotive** *in 1814, and he is often called the 'father of railways'. But he was not satisfied with his first efforts. He and his son worked together to design a lighter, more efficient locomotive. The result was the famous* Rocket, *which made its first journey in 1829.*

◀ When Victoria came to the throne, locomotives were still very much like the Rocket. The Stephensons' locomotive is shown here winning trials for the Liverpool and Manchester Railway. In a **tender** behind the driver, the Rocket carried its own coal and water to make the steam that drove its wheels. The Rocket had a top speed of 47 kilometres per hour, which was amazingly fast at this time.

▶ The railway industry expanded quickly. As well as providing better, cheaper transport, it created thousands of jobs. This engraving shows workers inside the circular **engine-house**, or roundhouse, at the Camden Town **depot** of the North Western Railway, in 1847. The huge engine-house was almost 50 metres across and could house 23 locomotives.

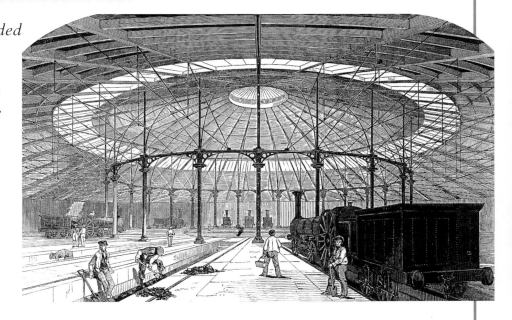

◀ Not everyone was happy with the railways. Many people found them frightening and thought that they ruined the peaceful countryside. Noisy steam locomotives also scared the horses and the hounds! Gentleman farmers look on in the background, perhaps in amusement.

ISAMBARD K BRUNEL

This great English engineer was born in Portsmouth in 1806. At the age of 17, after studying in Paris, Isambard Kingdom Brunel joined his father's business. Together they planned the first Thames Tunnel. The young Brunel was interested in railways and ships, as well as bridges and tunnels, and in 1833 he was appointed engineer to the Great Western Railway. His first major achievement was to design a new railway line from London to Bristol which opened in 1841. The following year Queen Victoria gave it her personal approval by travelling from Paddington to Slough on her way to Windsor Castle. Brunel went on to design and build great ships and bridges.

Brunel died in 1859 and never saw the completion of some of his greatest achievements. When he died, there were huge problems with his biggest ship, the *Great Eastern*, and the building of the Clifton **Suspension Bridge** in Bristol was stuck for lack of funds. But both the Clifton Bridge and the Royal Albert Bridge over the River Tamar were successfully completed and are still in use today.

► *Brunel (third from left) in 1857, watches an attempt to launch the biggest ship built up to that time. The* Great Eastern *was built with John Scott Russell (first left), at a* **shipyard** *on the River Thames. Several attempts were needed to launch the huge ship sideways into the river, because it had settled into the Thames mud. The* Great Eastern *finally took to the water in 1858.*

14

▲ Brunel's Great Eastern *had three forms of power – a four-bladed propeller, two paddle wheels driven by separate steam engines, and sails on six masts. The giant ship was 211 metres long and 26 metres wide. This was over twice as long as Brunel's ship, the* Great Britain, *which was the first propeller-driven ship to cross the Atlantic. The* Great Eastern *carried 15 000 tonnes of coal to fire its boilers, enough to steam to Australia without refuelling. It was used to lay the first* **telegraph cable** *across the Atlantic Ocean floor.*

▼ *The Clifton Suspension Bridge on the outskirts of Bristol. Money to build a bridge across this deep* **gorge** *in Avon was left by a Bristol man in 1753. At that time no engineer knew how to span the gorge. Almost 80 years later, Brunel won a design competition to build a suspension bridge. Building funds ran out and there was a long delay in completing the bridge, which was opened in December 1864. The bridge is 214 metres long and stands 79 metres above the River Avon. At the time it was the world's longest and highest suspension bridge.*

SHIPS

During the long reign of Queen Victoria steamships became more common and gradually took over from sailing ships. By 1840 paddle steamers were making regular voyages across the Atlantic Ocean between Britain and America. Yet towards the end of Victorian times the fastest and most successful cargo ships – clippers – were still driven by the wind.

Most ordinary Victorians only ever went on a long voyage if they decided to **emigrate** to another country, such as the United States or Australia. Many people emigrated to the **colonies** belonging to the British Empire. Most were poor families who wanted to leave Britain to find work and a decent standard of living.

In 1869 the voyage to Australia was made much easier and quicker by the opening of the Suez Canal. The canal was built through Egypt to connect the Mediterranean with the Red Sea and saved having to sail thousands of kilometres around the southern tip of Africa.

▲ *Some* **emigrants,** *such as these poor needlewomen, were encouraged to move to the colonies. Committees were set up to help workers and farmers to emigrate.*

This was cheaper than paying for them to be kept in **workhouses.** *The Australian government offered free transport to families with useful skills.*

► *The famous clipper the* Cutty Sark *made its* **maiden voyage** *in 1870. In full sail, it had a total of 34 sails on three tall masts, which made it very fast. This kind of ship was called a clipper because its speed allowed it to clip days off the sailing time of other ships. British clippers were mainly used to transport wool from Australia and tea from China. The* Cutty Sark *sailed at over 30 kilometres an hour. It is now kept as a museum in London.*

▼ *In Victorian times warships did not look very different from most cargo and passenger vessels. By the middle of the nineteenth century, however, wooden warships were proving to be no match for the latest guns and shells. The British wanted to defend their country and empire against attack,* and so they launched new 'ironclad' ships with armour plating. This ship, HMS Nelson, was launched in 1880. It was powered by both steam and sail, or a combination of the two, and had 12 heavy guns. The Nelson was 85 metres long, with a top speed of 26 kilometres per hour.

POSTAL SERVICE

Stagecoaches had been carrying sealed letters around Britain since the late 1700s, but before Victorian times there was no national system. Then in 1837, the year that Victoria became queen, a retired schoolteacher named Rowland Hill wrote a detailed **pamphlet** calling for a single, cheap postage rate.

Hill suggested that postage should be paid in advance by the sender of the letter, with a stamp stuck on the envelope to show that postage had been paid. He wanted the single postal rate for ordinary letters to cover the whole of Great Britain, with heavier letters and parcels costing more.

This idea was accepted by **parliament**, and in 1840 the world's first postage stamp, the penny black, was printed and issued. The new system was very popular and improved communication across the country. By 1855 pillar boxes were appearing in the streets, and a lot of post was carried across the country by train.

▼ *Mail coaches struggling through the snow near Manchester, around 1840. As well as letters, the coaches also carried fare-paying passengers. Gradually more coaches were added to the expanding railways so that they could carry the extra mail, with a special Royal Mail guard to watch over the post.*

► As her father wanders off reading his letter, a young woman hopes the postman has a letter for her, too. Receiving a letter was an important and exciting event in the days before telephones. People kept in touch with family and friends outside their village or town by letter writing. The village postman usually posted his letters on foot. If he had a long round, he would ride a horse.

▼ The Victorians were great inventors, and they soon thought up ways of speeding up the post. Here the mailbags are being sent from Euston Station in London to a **sorting office** half a kilometre away, by a **pneumatic** tube. The system worked by blowing air through the 76-centimetre wide tube to move the small carriages full of mail. Mail took just three minutes to travel from an arriving train to the sorting office. The idea was a huge success.

THE OMNIBUS

The Latin word *omnibus* means 'for all', and in the early nineteenth century the word came to be used for large carriages which carried the public from place to place. In later years the word was shortened to bus, which we still use today.

Unlike today's buses, the first omnibuses had no engine; they were pulled along by pairs of horses. The single carriages soon became **double-deckers** with a covered downstairs compartment and an open top.

Later, many towns laid tramlines through the busy streets, and trams replaced many omnibuses, although to begin with they were still pulled along by horses. By the end of the nineteenth century, horse power was gradually replaced by steam, electric and finally petrol engines.

▶ *This illustration of a new type of omnibus was published in 1851. Many passengers found the first omnibuses crowded and uncomfortable. This new design aimed to solve these problems. All passengers had their own enclosed seat instead of sharing a bench, and a speaking tube to tell the* **conductor** *when to stop. The inventor added: 'Should any person wish to speak to his neighbour, he has only to touch a spring, and there will open a window for that purpose.' Each omnibus also had a special device which counted the number of passengers carried each day.*

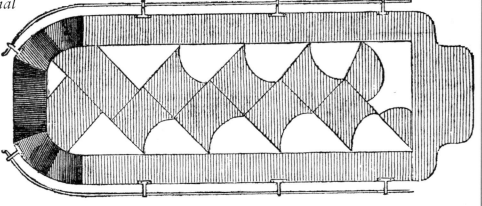

◄ In this traffic jam in the 1890s omnibuses queue up near a bus stop in Charing Cross, London. The horses' tails were **docked** so that they would not be caught in the shafts or wheels. By this time companies had realized that buses were a good form of moving advertisement. An omnibus ride cost two or three old pence, about one penny in today's money.

► Horses pull trams along Royal Avenue, Belfast, in the 1890s. There are lots of pedestrians on the wide pavements and a few carts and carriages on the **cobbled** road. Trams generally drove down the middle of the road, which helped traffic and other road users.

► The Pioneer omnibus was first introduced in Edinburgh in 1871. It had a steam engine and long benches for passengers to sit on top. The fares board outside states that a seat on the outside bench cost 2d (d was the old sign for pence), while a ride inside cost 3d.

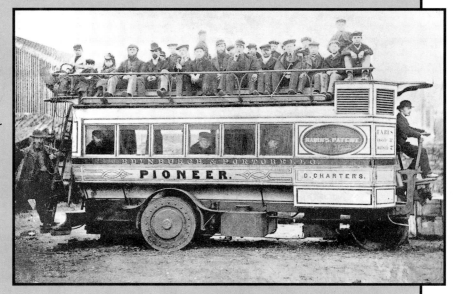

BICYCLES

Early forms of bicycles without pedals existed before the Victorian age. In 1839, a Scottish blacksmith, Kirkpatrick Macmillan, added rods to the back wheel of the bicycle. Each rod had a foot crank that the rider pushed back and forth to drive the back wheel. Before long, rotating pedals moved to the front wheel.

Bicycles were not very well known until 1870 when the penny-farthing, also known as an ordinary or a high-wheeler, was developed. In the next 15 years, 200 000 penny-farthings were manufactured. But they were not easy to ride, especially for women who wore long skirts.

In 1885 the English inventor and bicycle manufacturer, James Starley, produced the first successful safety bicycle, which had wheels the same size and a chain connecting the pedals to the back wheel. This design took bikes through to the end of the century and is still the one used today.

▲ *The huge front wheel of a penny-farthing was up to 1.5 metres high. There were no gears, and the penny-farthing travelled a long distance with a single turn of the pedals. A book published in the 1880s described how to get off a penny-farthing: 'To dismount, the rider slackens his speed, and just as the pedal reaches its lowest point, he throws the opposite leg backwards over the* **backbone**, *putting most of his weight on the pedal and handles. The danger to the* **novice** *lies in the fact that the machine may "kick" and send him over the handles'.*

▼ *Tricycles were easier to ride and safer than bicycles in horse-drawn traffic. They were particularly popular with women, though many people thought them too manly and sporty for the 'fair sex'. This picture was printed in the* Illustrated London News *in 1892, as part of an article criticizing women's* **emancipation** *as being unnatural and unnecessary. The article was written by a woman.*

THE

Safety Skirt Holder

PATENT Nº 22437

PRICE **ONE** SHILLING

WITHOUT SKIRT HOLDER   WITH SKIRT HOLDER

Victorian women were not supposed to show too much of their legs, or even their ankles. This made cycling difficult, and they also had the problem of getting a long skirt caught in the chain or wheel-spokes.

The skirt holder was designed to help women deal with these problems. It cost one shilling, or five new pence, and was attached to the front of the bicycle. It held the skirt down so that it didn't flap about.

By the end of the 1890s cycling was already being taken seriously as a sport. Special tracks were built, such as this one shown in 1897. Bikes developed quickly from slow **boneshakers** to light racing machines. There were cycle races for men in the first modern Olympic Games, held in Athens, Greece, in 1896. Women did not have their own races until almost a hundred years later.

THE UNDERGROUND

The world's first underground trains ran in London in 1863. By this time traffic had become a real problem in the nation's capital, with horse-drawn vehicles choking the streets.

Railways had made long-distance travel between towns easier, and one of the great advantages of the London underground railway was that it connected the city's mainline stations, such as King's Cross, Paddington and Victoria. These stations became connecting stops on the new Metropolitan Railway.

The original trains used steam locomotives, specially built to be low and squat, but they caused problems by filling the tunnels with smoke and steam. By 1890 they had been replaced by electric trains, similar to those that still run today. In 1896, the world's first underground cable railway opened in Glasgow. Moving cables pulled trains along so that there was no smoke or steam.

▼ *In the early 1860s the first underground railway in London was built. A big trench was dug and the railway track was laid. A roof was built over the track and earth was put back on top of it. The tunnel was over six metres wide and five metres high. Many* *roads were dug up and rebuilt, and houses that were in the way were pulled down. The problem at this station, King's Cross, was an underground river full of **sewage**. This was enclosed in a huge iron pipe, so that the new trains could run underneath it.*

► *Important people, including the Chancellor of the Exchequer and later prime minister William Gladstone, took trial trips on the London underground in 1862. You can see the steam locomotive pulling the open carriages, which look like cattle trucks. The real coaches were closed and much more comfortable.*

▼ *A train approaches Baker Street station in the 1860s. This was one of 25 stops on the Metropolitan Inner-Circle Railway. Later, the Victorians built more underground lines by digging much deeper. They worked inside a metal tube that stopped the earth from collapsing into the tunnel as the* digging went on, 18 metres below the surface. The narrower, rounder tunnels had cast-iron linings and gave the underground network the nickname the tube. The first new coaches had no windows, because engineers thought that passengers might be frightened by the view – or lack of it!

RAIL NETWORK

The railway was the great transport success of Victorian times. Brunel's Great Western Railway, or GWR, was soon nicknamed 'God's Wonderful Railway'. By 1850 trains were travelling the 190 kilometres between London and Bristol in two and a half hours.

But as the rail network grew and spread across the whole country, steps had to be taken to make sure that the track was standard so that all the trains could run on the same track. Brunel had used a wider **gauge** than other companies. In 1869, ten years after Brunel's death, work began on relaying the GWR track with a narrower gauge. It took 23 years altogether, and was completed by a workforce of over 4000 men.

Many of the new rail lines needed long bridges and tunnels and during Victorian times engineers designed and began to build bridges across the country. In 1890 the Forth Bridge opened which helped to take hours off the train journey north of Edinburgh.

◄ *After 1870 Britain's ports also became important railway stations, linking trains with ships. The railway station, harbour and pier at Dover was planned for the first cross-channel rail ferry to France. Engineers had already thought of digging a tunnel under the English Channel, but decided against it. Instead, they decided to use special lifting equipment at Dover, to transfer trains, including passengers and their luggage, from the railway to the steamer.*

► *As the rail network grew, travelling by train became easier and more comfortable. In 1879 the Great Northern Railway added dining cars to their trains. These were luxurious carriages with a first-class menu. Naturally they were expensive, and only well-off passengers could afford to eat in them. The GNR also offered the first British railway carriage with a side corridor. At each end of the carriage there was a lavatory, one for ladies and one for gentlemen.*

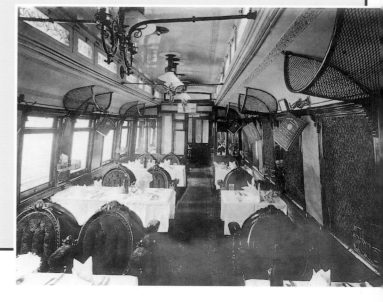

◄ By 1899, when this poster was printed, the rail network covered the whole country. Passengers could visit Windermere in the Lake District, or Llandudno in north Wales. The Britannia Bridge across the Menai Straits to Anglesey, built by the great railway engineer, Robert Stephenson, was opened in 1850. For journeys further afield, the port of Holyhead connected rail travellers with a steamship to Ireland, and from Liverpool they could even catch a ship bound for New York.

◄ The Tay Bridge across the Firth of Tay in Scotland was completed in 1878. Soon afterwards, Queen Victoria crossed the bridge in her royal train. She was so impressed that she **knighted** the designer of the bridge, Sir Thomas Bouch. But on a stormy day the following year, disaster struck. Severe gales blew down a section of the bridge as a passenger train was crossing. The train plunged into the river below, and the 75 people on board died. Boats searched for survivors, but none was found.

HORSELESS CARRIAGES

The end of the Victorian age saw a new form of transport that would soon change everybody's idea of travel: the motor car. The first petrol-driven car went on sale to the public in 1885. It was a three-wheeler, built and sold by Karl Benz in Germany.

This new technology spread rapidly, and British engineers and businessmen brought the new cars from Europe and began developing their own models. The first cars looked like horse-drawn carriages without the horses, which is why they were called horseless carriages.

The first cars were very expensive and only rich people could afford to buy them. The cars were very dirty and noisy. They were not covered, so driver and passengers generally rode in the open exposed to the wind and rain. Drivers wore **goggles** to keep dirt and dust out of their eyes. At first all the drivers were men. Women passengers wore hats with veils to protect them from the weather and dust.

▲ *Before 1896, a law stated that all 'road locomotives' should have two drivers and a person walking ahead of the vehicle with a red flag to warn of its approach. The speed limit of three kilometres per hour kept cars in pace with the flag-man.*

This photograph shows Charles Stewart Rolls driving a French car in the early 1890s. A few years later, Rolls met Henry Royce and they formed one of the most famous luxury car companies in the world, Rolls-Royce.

► *The Automobile Club was formed in 1897, and the first London motor show was held the following year. This advertisement of 1899 shows some of the strange motorized contraptions that were on offer at the time.*

▼ *For many people motoring was a pleasant pastime. Those fortunate and wealthy enough to own a car liked to take it out for a run, just for the fun of it. It was some years before the introduction of mass production meant that motor cars could be afforded by most ordinary people.*

Glossary

backbone the bar connecting the two wheels of a penny-farthing bicycle.

boneshaker an old bicycle with solid tyres that was uncomfortable to ride.

cobbled made up of cobblestones: small, round stones used as a road surface.

colony a country which is ruled by another country.

conductor a person who collects the passengers' fares on a bus.

cutting a channel cut through high ground for a railway track or a road.

depot a large area where buses and trains are kept when they are not in use.

dock to cut an animal's tail short.

double-decker a bus which has an upstairs and a downstairs.

emancipation freedom to do and behave as you want within the law.

embankment an earth or stone bank that carries a railway track or a road.

emigrant a person who emigrates.

emigrate to leave your own country to go and live in another country.

engine-house a building where railway engines or locomotives are kept.

gauge the distance between the rails of a railway track.

goggles special glasses worn to protect the eyes from dirt and dust.

gorge a steep, narrow valley, usually with a stream or river running through it.

hearse a car that carries the coffin to a funeral.

hydraulic operated by using the pressure of a liquid such as oil or water.

industrial to do with industry and manufacturing. Industrial goods are made in factories.

invalid a person who is ill or disabled.

knight a special title given to someone by the king or queen.

lock a section of a river or canal that is closed off by gates so that the water level can be raised or lowered to let boats go through.

locomotive an engine that pulls a train along a railway track.

maiden voyage a ship's first journey at sea.

novice an inexperienced beginner.

paddle-steamer a ship that is pushed through the water by large paddle wheels driven by a steam engine.

pamphlet a small booklet containing information.

parliament the place where a country's laws are made. The British parliament is in London.

patent to register an invention so that no-one else can copy it and sell it as their own.

pneumatic operated by using the pressure of air.

port a town with a harbour where ships can load and unload.

sewage waste matter carried from homes and businesses in pipes called sewers.

shanks' pony a phrase that means walking on your own legs.

shipyard a place where ships are built and repaired.

sorting office a place where letters are sorted into their postal areas before being delivered.

suspension bridge a bridge that is suspended, or hangs, from strong metal cables.

telegraph cable a thick wire rope along which electrical signals can be sent.

tender a wagon attached to the back of a steam locomotive that carries fuel and water.

toll a charge that has to be paid to use a road or bridge.

trap a small two-wheeled carriage, usually pulled by a single pony.

viaduct a long, high bridge with a series of arches that carries a railway track or a road.

workhouse a place where poor people received food and accommodation in return for work.

Index

advertisements 9, 21, 29
Atlantic Ocean 15, 16
Australia 15, 16, 17
Automobile Club 29

Baker Street station 25
barges 10
Belfast 21
Benz, Karl 28
bicycles 4, 22-23
boats 10-11
Bouch, Sir Thomas 27
bridges 11, 12, 14, 15, 26, 27
Bristol 14, 15, 26
Brunel, Isambard Kingdom 14-15, 26
buses 6, 20-21
bus stops 21

cabs 8, 9
canals 10-11
carriages 4, 5, 7, 8, 9, 20, 21, 28
carrier's wagon 6
carts 7, 9, 21
classes of travel 12, 26
Clifton suspension bridge 14-15
clippers 16-17
coaches & coach houses 7
coal 7, 13, 15
colonies 16
comfort 6, 7, 12, 20, 21, 25, 26, 28
communication 18-19
cost of transport 6, 7, 8, 12, 13, 21, 26, 28, 29
countryside 6, 13
Crewe 5
Cutty Sark 17
cycle races 23

double-decker omnibuses 20
Dover 26

Edinburgh 21, 26
electric trains 24
emancipation 22
emigration 16
engineers & engineering 6, 10, 11, 14-15, 26, 27, 28

engine-houses 13
English Channel 26
Euston station 19

farms & farmers 7, 13, 16
ferries 11, 26
Forth Bridge 26

gauge 26
Gladstone, William 25
Glasgow 24
goods 6, 7, 9, 10, 11, 12
Grand Union Canal 11
Great Britain (a ship) 15
Great Eastern (a ship) 14-15
Great Exhibition 8
Great Northern Railway 26
Great Western Railway 14, 26

hackney carriages 8
hansom cabs 9
Hansom, Joseph 9
hearses 8
Hill, Rowland 18
hiring transport 7, 8
Holyhead 27
horseless carriages 5, 28-29
horses & horse-drawn transport 4, 6-7, 8, 9, 10, 13, 19, 20, 21, 22, 24

industry 8, 11, 13
invalid carriages 8
inventors 19, 20, 22
Irish Sea 11
ironclad ships 17

jobs & work 6, 13, 16

King's Cross station 24

laws 12, 28
Liverpool 12, 27
Liverpool and Manchester Railway 13
locks 10, 11
London 5, 8, 9, 11, 12, 14, 17, 19, 21, 24, 25, 26, 29

Macmillan, Kirkpatrick 22
mail - see 'postal service'

Manchester 11, 12, 18
Manchester Ship Canal 11
mass production 29
McAdam, John Loudon 6
Metropolitan Inner-Circle Railway 24-25
motor cars 5, 28-29
motor shows 29

narrow boats 11
navvies 10
North Western Railway 13

omnibuses 4, 5, 20-21

Paddington station 14, 24
paddle steamers 11, 16
pedestrians 6, 21
penny black 18
penny-farthings 22
petrol engine & petrol-driven transport 6, 20, 28-29
Pioneer omnibus 21
poor people 7, 16
ports 11, 26, 27
Portsmouth 13
postal service 4, 18-19
public transport 12, 20-21

Queen Victoria 4, 5, 6, 13, 14, 16, 17, 27

rail ferries 26
railways 4, 5, 6, 10, 11, 12-13, 14, 24-27
railway towns 5
Regent's Canal 11
rich people 8, 26, 28, 29
River Avon 15
River Humber 11
River Mersey 11
River Tamar 14
River Thames 11, 14
river transport 10-11
River Weaver 10
roads 4, 6, 7, 8, 10, 21, 24
Rocket 12-13
Rolls, Charles Stewart 28
Royal Albert Bridge 14
Royal Mail 18

Royce, Henry 28
Russell, John Scott 14

sailing ships 15, 16-17
shanks' pony 6
ships 14-17, 26
Slough 14
speed of transport 8, 12, 13, 16, 17, 26, 28
stagecoaches 4, 7, 18
Starley, James 22
stations 5, 8, 24-25, 26
steam 13, 17, 24
steam engines 6, 10, 15, 20, 21
steam ferries 11
steam locomotives 12-13, 24, 25
steamships 15, 16-17, 26, 27
Stephenson, George 12-13
Stephenson, Robert 12-13, 27
Suez Canal 16

taxis 8
Tay Bridge 26, 27
tea 17
tolls 7
towns 4, 5, 6, 8-9, 19, 20, 24
towpaths 10
traffic 5, 6, 9, 21, 22, 24
traffic lights 8
trains 4, 6, 12-13, 18, 19, 24, 26-27
trams 4, 5, 20, 21
traps 9
Trent and Mersey Canal 10
tricycles 22
tube 25
tunnels 12, 14, 24-25, 26

underground railway 5, 24-25

viaducts 12
Victoria station 24

walking 6
warships 17
waterways 10-11